P9-CBI-913

HORSES

The
TENNESSEE WALKING
Horse

by Lori Coleman

Consultant:
DeAnn Weston
Tennessee Walking Horse Breeders' and
Exhibitors' Association (TWHBEA)
Lewisburg, Tennessee

Capstone press

Mankato, Minnesota

Edge Books are published by Capstone Press,
151 Good Counsel Drive, P.O. Box 669, Mankato, Minnesota 56002.
www.capstonepress.com

Library of Congress Cataloging-in-Publication Data
Coleman, Lori.
    The Tennessee walking horse / by Lori Coleman.
        p. cm.—(Edge Books. Horses)
    Summary: "Describes the Tennessee Walking Horse, including its history,
physical features, and uses today"—Provided by publisher.
    Includes bibliographical references (p. 31) and index.
    ISBN-13: 978-0-7368-5461-0 (hardcover)
    ISBN-10: 0-7368-5461-4 (hardcover)
    1. Tennessee walking horse—Juvenile literature. I. Title. II. Series.
SF293.T4C65 2006
636.1'3—dc22   2005017574

Editorial Credits
Carrie A. Braulick, editor; Juliette Peters, set designer; Bobbi J. Dey, book
    designer; Deirdre Barton, photo researcher/photo editor

Photo Credits
Bob Langrish, cover, back cover, 11, 13, 14, 16–17, 19, 20, 22, 23, 29
Capstone Press/Gary Sundermeyer (objects), 12; Karon Dubke, 7, 15, 21
Graphics by Loita, 27
Jack Greene Photography, 25
Mary Evans Picture Library, 5
Photo furnished by TWHBEA, 6, 9

1 2 3 4 5 6 11 10 09 08 07 06

Table of Contents

FEATURES

Chapter 1

Tennessee Pride

About 200 years ago, U.S. settlers began pouring into the new state of Tennessee. Forests and large areas of rough, rocky land greeted the settlers.

Soon, horse breeders in Tennessee had a common goal. They wanted a comfortable riding horse that could carry them easily over the rough land. The scene was set for the Tennessee Walking Horse to appear.

Many Horses

During the 1800s, settlers in Tennessee rode many types of horses. They rode Morgans, Canadian Pacers, and Narragansett Pacers.

Learn about:
- ★ A common goal
- ★ Bald Stockings
- ★ Black Allan

4

The use of horses for travel in the early 1800s created a demand for comfortable riding horses.

▼Tennessee Walkers were bred to easily carry riders over rough land.

Morgans were small and strong. Canadian and Narragansett Pacers were especially comfortable to ride.

Thoroughbreds were one of the most popular breeds in Tennessee. People first brought these tall, fast horses to North America in the early 1700s.

A Smooth Ride

Tennessee horse breeders worked hard to create the best riding horses possible. They bred Morgans, Canadian Pacers, and Narragansett Pacers together. They also added Thoroughbreds and their close relatives, Standardbreds, to the mix. Ancestors of the tall, graceful American Saddlebred were also used for breeding.

Soon, the breeders' work paid off. Their sturdy horses walked with ease up and down the rocky hills of Tennessee.

The Running Walk

In 1837, a stallion like no other was born in Tennessee. His name was Bald Stockings. This horse had an unusual gait. When he increased his speed at a walk, he didn't start trotting. Instead, he kept walking, but much faster. This smooth gait became known as the running walk.

Tennessee horse breeders knew the smooth running walk would make their horses even more valuable. They mated Bald Stockings with their mares. Horses that could do the running walk were first known as Southern Plantation Walking Horses or Tennessee Pacers.

By the mid-1880s, people in other states had heard about the easy-to-ride horses in Tennessee. They bought many Southern Plantation Walking Horses. People rode the horses from town to town and used them to pull farm equipment.

The First Tennessee Walkers

In 1886, a black horse named Black Allan was born in Kentucky. His father was a Standardbred known for his fast trot in harness races. His mother was a Morgan. Black Allan disappointed many of his first owners. They wanted a harness racer that could trot fast. But Black Allan preferred to do the running walk.

In 1903, Black Allan's new owner, James Brantley, realized the value of Black Allan's running walk. He bred Black Allan with Southern Plantation Walking Horses. Black Allan's offspring also had his running walk. Black Allan and his foals became the first Tennessee Walking Horses.

An Official Breed

In 1935, Tennessee horse breeders formed the Tennessee Walking Horse Breeders' Association of America. Owners registered their horses' breeding records with the group. Today, this registry is known as the Tennessee Walking Horse Breeders' and Exhibitors' Association (TWHBEA). It has about 430,000 registered horses.

Midnight Sun

Midnight Sun started his show career later than most Tennessee Walkers. But his winning record quickly earned him great fame. Midnight Sun was born in 1940. In 1945 and 1946, he was named the World Grand Champion at the Tennessee Walking Horse National Celebration. Many of Midnight Sun's foals also were World Champions, and his descendants continue to win the same titles. A statue of Midnight Sun stands at the TWHBEA headquarters in Lewisburg, Tennessee.

Chapter 2

A Step Above the Rest

The Tennessee Walking Horse's smooth running walk attracts many people to the breed. Yet these horses have even more to offer. Tennessee Walkers seem to have the best qualities of all the breeds in their ancestry. Their graceful appearance and friendly, gentle personalities are well known.

Size

Tennessee Walkers are average-sized horses. Horses are measured in hands. Each hand equals 4 inches (10 centimeters). Most Tennessee Walkers stand between 15 and 17 hands tall from the ground to the top of the shoulders, or withers.

Learn about:
★ Main features
★ An assortment of colors
★ The running walk

Tennessee Walking Horses are both muscular and graceful.

11

Appearance

Tennessee Walkers look both stylish and strong. Their necks are long, arched, and muscular. Tennessee Walkers have slender legs, short backs, wide chests, and muscular hindquarters. Sloped shoulders give the horses a long stride. Tennessee Walkers usually have long, thick manes and tails.

People who want a horse have many choices to make. If they want a Tennessee Walker, deciding what color they want their horse to be is sure to be difficult.

Tennessee Walking Horses can have nearly any coat color. Common colors are chestnut, black, bay, and roan. The copper color of a chestnut Tennessee Walker is like a new penny. Bay horses are brown. They have black manes, tails, and lower legs. Roan horses have a dark coat color with a mixture of white hairs.

Many people like the look of overo and tobiano Tennessee Walkers. These horses have white spots or patches.

↓ Some overo Tennessee Walkers have white spots on black coats.

Tennessee Walkers overstride during the running walk.

Gaits

Tennessee Walkers have longer back legs than other breeds do. This feature causes the Tennessee Walker to overstride. When the horse walks, its back foot reaches farther forward than the spot where the front foot had been.

An overstride helps give the Tennessee Walker its unique gaits.

The Tennessee Walker's main gaits are the flat-foot walk, the running walk, and the canter. The flat-foot walk is a fairly fast gait. The horse overstrides while keeping its back feet close to the ground. The horse's head bobs as it steps.

The running walk is faster than the flat-foot walk. The back legs reach even farther forward than they do in the flat-foot walk. The horse keeps bobbing its head as it steps. Sometimes the horse even clicks its teeth to the rhythm.

Some people call the Tennessee Walking Horse's canter the "rocking-chair gait." Like a rocking chair, the canter has a smooth rise-and-fall motion.

A Kind Personality

Tennessee Walkers have many of the same qualities that a person would want a good friend to have. The horses are known for their good manners. They are friendly, gentle, and reliable.

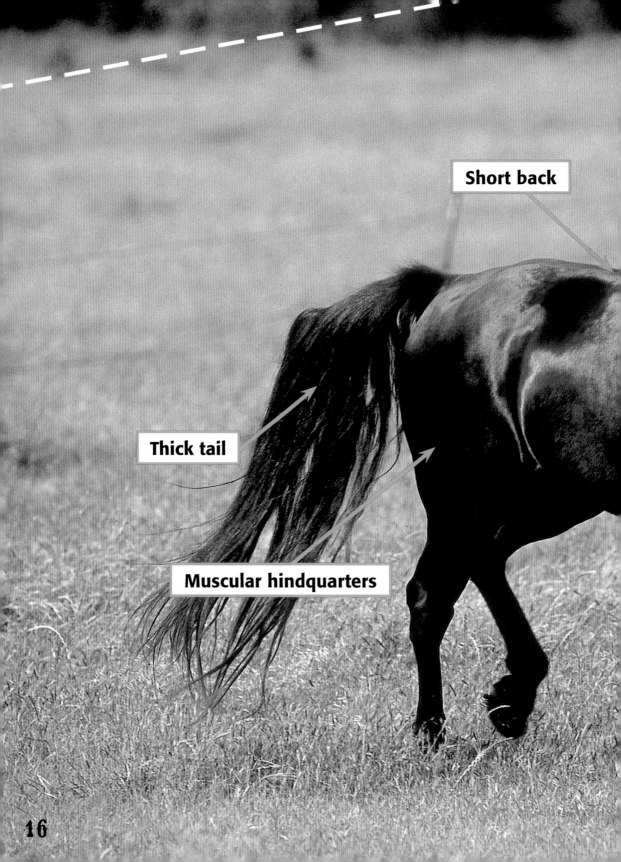

Short back

Thick tail

Muscular hindquarters

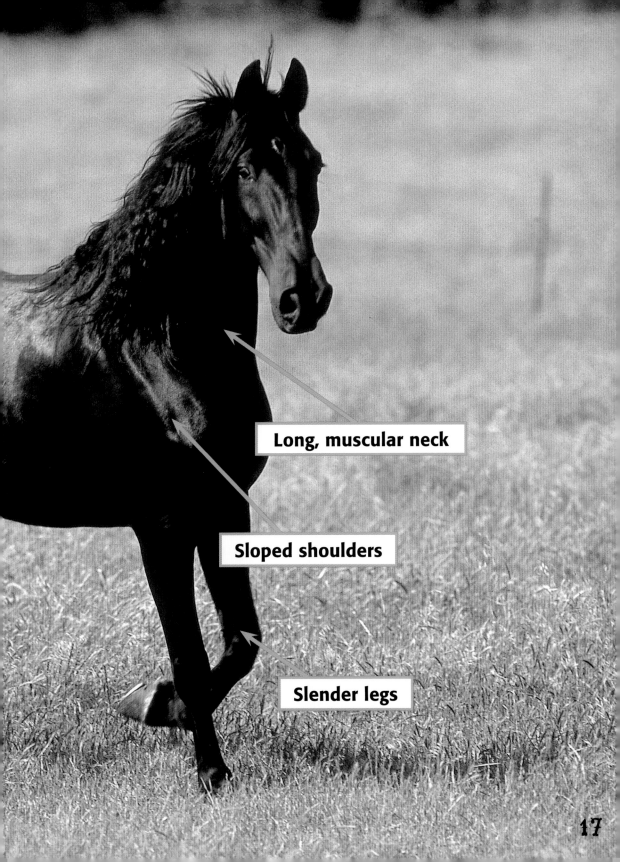

Long, muscular neck

Sloped shoulders

Slender legs

In the Show Ring

By the 1930s, people used tractors for fieldwork and cars for transportation. Many horse owners then began competing with their horses in shows.

In 1939, the first Tennessee Walking Horse National Celebration was held in Shelbyville, Tennessee. Judges at the show awarded the first World Grand Champion title to Strolling Jim. Today, this 11-day show is the largest Tennessee Walker show in the United States. Tennessee Walkers also compete in many smaller shows throughout North America.

Learn about:
- ★ Strolling Jim
- ★ Performance and pleasure classes
- ★ Water glass classes

18

People train their Tennessee Walkers to lift their front feet high during shows.

19

NHSC Shows

The National Horse Show Commission (NHSC) approves shows for Tennessee Walkers in at least 21 states. Horses competing in these shows must be registered with the TWHBEA.

Tennessee Walking Horse shows are divided into performance and pleasure classes. In performance classes, horses wear large shoes and perform high-stepping, lively gaits. In pleasure classes, the shoes are smaller and the gaits are less lively.

▲ Tennessee Walkers that compete in performance classes wear large shoes.

Classes are divided based on the age of the horse and rider. Separate classes also are held for professionals and amateurs.

Versatility Program

Some Tennessee Walking Horses compete in the TWHBEA's versatility program. Shows in this program have a wider variety of classes than other shows.

Versatility shows may include trail, driving, and jumping classes. In trail classes, horses maneuver around obstacles. In driving classes, a horse wears a harness that connects it to a cart.

Many riders enjoy competing in water glass classes. In these events, riders hold a glass of water while moving at different gaits. The rider who has the most water in the glass at the end of the class wins. Participants in the versatility program earn points at each show. At the end of the season, the competitors with the most points receive awards.

FACT
In the 1940s and 1950s, actor Roy Rogers rode a Tennessee Walker known as "Trigger." Trigger's popularity helped interest in the breed grow.

Trainers work to make the gaits of Tennessee Walkers perfect for shows.

Training

People who compete in Tennessee Walker shows spend a lot of time training their horses. Young foals learn to wear a halter and walk with a handler. They also learn to behave well around people. Tennessee Walkers are ready to be ridden when they are about 2 years old.

People training horses for pleasure and performance classes ride the horses often. Riding regularly helps the horses build up strength. Over time, the horses also become more relaxed while being ridden. Tennessee Walkers have a more noticeable head bob when they are relaxed.

⬇ Training begins soon after foals are born.

23

Tennessee Walking Horses in Action

Tennessee Walking Horse fans make Shelbyville, Tennessee, a busy place at the end of every summer. About 250,000 people gather there to watch the National Celebration. About 2,000 horses compete at the show each year. Winning horses receive World Grand Champion titles.

Other Uses

Not all Tennessee Walking Horse owners compete at shows just for Tennessee Walkers. Some shows are for all horse breeds. Other shows are only for gaited horses. Gaited horses can perform a gait other than the walk, trot, and canter.

Learn about:
- ★ **National Celebration**
- ★ **Field trials**
- ★ **Growth of the breed**

In 2004, The Black Night Shade became the World Grand Champion.

Tennessee Walking Horses are the most popular horses in field trials. Field trials are competitions for bird hunting dogs. The dog handlers ride horses to keep track of their dogs from a distance. Handlers especially like Tennessee Walkers because they are comfortable and calm.

All riders can enjoy the Tennessee Walker's smooth gaits. But people with back injuries or other physical problems may appreciate them even more. Many Tennessee Walkers are used in riding programs for people with disabilities.

Owning a Tennessee Walker

Owning a Tennessee Walking Horse is a big responsibility. Like all horses, Tennessee Walkers need food, water, and shelter. Horses also need regular veterinary and hoof care.

Even though horse ownership is hard work, owners of Tennessee Walkers know the work is worth it. With their smooth gaits and cooperative personalities, it is easy to see why the number of Tennessee Walkers in North America continues to grow.

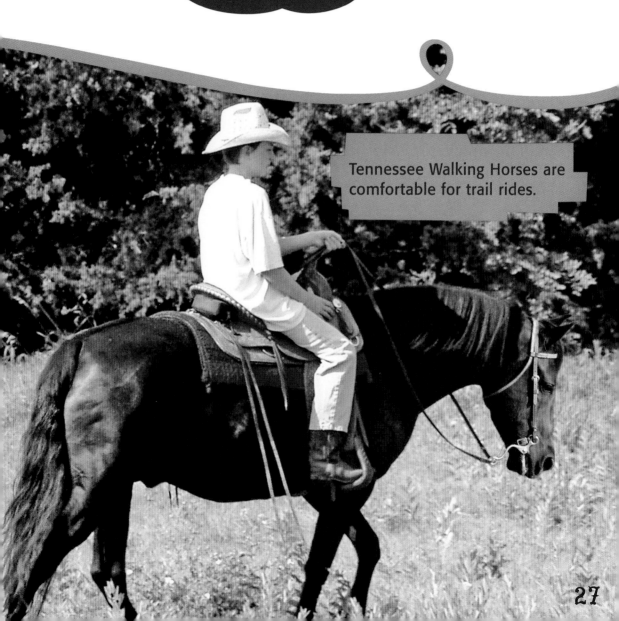

Tennessee Walking Horses are comfortable for trail rides.

Fast Facts:
The Tennessee Walking Horse

History: Tennessee Walking Horses were first bred in Tennessee in the late 1880s. They have Narragansett Pacer, Canadian Pacer, Thoroughbred, Morgan, and American Saddlebred ancestry.

Height: Tennessee Walkers are 15 to 17 hands (about 5 feet or 1.5 meters) tall at the withers. Each hand equals 4 inches (10 centimeters).

Weight: 900 to 1,200 pounds (400 to 540 kilograms)

Colors: Tennessee Walkers can be one of many colors. Common colors are bay, black, chestnut, and roan.

Features: short back; wide chest; slim legs; sloped shoulders; long, muscular neck; strong hindquarters; thick, long manes and tails

Personality: calm, friendly, cooperative

Abilities: Tennessee Walkers show off their running walk at horse shows. They also are excellent trail riding horses.

Life span: about 25 years

Glossary

amateur (AM-uh-chur)—a person who does not earn a living from competing in a sport

field trial (FEELD TRYE-uhl)—a competition among bird hunting dogs

gait (GATE)—the manner in which a horse moves

mare (MAIR)—an adult female horse

overstride (oh-vur-STRYDE)—to reach the back foot farther forward than the place where the front foot had been

registry (REH-juh-stree)—an organization that keeps track of the ancestry for horses of a certain breed

rhythm (RITH-uhm)—a regular beat; Tennessee Walking Horses bob their heads to the rhythm of their steps.

stallion (STAL-yuhn)—an adult male horse that can be used for breeding

Read More

Gentle, Victor, and Janet Perry. *Tennessee Walking Horses.* Great American Horses. Milwaukee: Gareth Stevens, 2001.

Gruber, Beth. *Horse Sense.* Pet's Point of View. Minneapolis: Compass Point Books, 2005.

Kimball, Cheryl. *Horse Showing for Kids.* North Adams, Mass.: Storey Kids, 2004.

Internet Sites

FactHound offers a safe, fun way to find Internet sites related to this book. All of the sites on FactHound have been researched by our staff.

Here's how:

1. Visit *www.facthound.com*
2. Type in this special code **0736854614** for age-appropriate sites. Or enter a search word related to this book for a more general search.
3. Click on the **Fetch It** button.

FactHound will fetch the best sites for you!

Index